W9-ALG-402

THE CAPTAIN UNDERPANTS Super-Silly STiCKeR STUDiO

HI EVERYBODY. GEORGE AND I ARE EXCITED TO HAVE YOU AT THE STUDIO.

THIS IS MORE THAN JUST A BOOK FULL OF STICKERS. IT'S A BOOK OF STICKER ACTION. CHECK OUT ALL YOU CAN DO!

KLUTZ

CAPTAIN UNDERPANTS AND HIS WORLD
CREATED BY **DAV PILKEY**

HOW TO USE THIS BOOK

DIRECTIONS ON THIS SIDE **STICKERS ON THIS SIDE**

TO START, COMBINE AND COLOR PICTURES FROM SHEET #1 WITH WORDS FROM SHEET #2.

#2

WEDGIE POWER!

FASTER THAN A SPEEDING WAISTBAND

TRA-LA-LAAAA!

GAME OVER, BUB!

TRUTH! JUSTICE!

AND ALL THINGS PRE-SHRUNK AND COTTONY

GEORGE & HAROLD

are always on the run! Color these creative kids and their skateboards, then combine them to show off some skateboard trickery.

#3

And, we've included a few

GLOWING HYPNO-RINGS

to get you out of trouble!

On sticker sheet #4, break out the green, brown, and yellow markers.

#4

Time to color some

SCARY STUFF,

including the scariest of all things...cafeteria food.

RUMPER STICKERS #5

These stickers are built for rear viewing. You may wear them yourself, OR, to share the fun, set them on a chair... sticky side up.

SET THE TRAP

SNACK ATTACKS #6

Improve your snacks with the stickers on sheet #6!

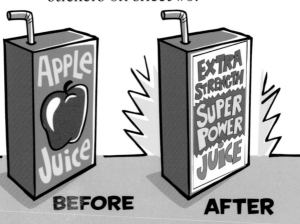

Apple Juice

EXTRA STRENGTH SUPER POWER JUICE

BEFORE **AFTER**

#5

PANTS PROTECTED BY

CONTENTS UNDER PRESSURE

THIS END UP

BLAST ZONE

BACK OFF! NO TAILGATING

My UnderPants Were UnderPants of the Month AT JEROME HORWITZ Elementary School

I BRAKE FOR ZOMBIE NERDS

#6

CREAM OF BOOGER FLAVOR

WORM GUTS FLAVOR

STINKY SOCK FLAVOR

SUPER EVIL RAPID GROWTH JUICE

SPICY TOE JAM FLAVOR

ZOMBIE NERD JUICE

EXTRA STRENGTH SUPER POWER JUICE

HiDDEN MESSAGES #7

These stickers say one thing when the lights are on, but something else when the lights go off.

TALKiNG TOiLETS AND SURPRiSE EYES #8

Place the stickers on sheet #8 all around the bathroom for more surprises when the lights go off!

STicKeR SCieNCE

~ with ~

MELViN SNEEDLY

#9 AND #10

GET READY TO
BE AMAZED BY THESE
INCREDIBLE STICKER
SIMULATIONS OF WHAT
IT'S LIKE TO BE ME.

STICKERBOT

Grab a sheet of paper and build your own sticker robot.

#9

FOR EXAMPLE:

COMBINE-O-TRON TEST DRIVE

#10

The teachers at Jerome Horwitz Elementary are usually pretty mixed up. But why not REALLY mix them up by swapping their heads?

#9

#10

Use the charts below to find your and your friends' SILLY NAMES. Then, make name tags!

FIRST CHART: Use the first letter of your first NAME To Determine Your **NEW** First NAME!

A = Stinky	J = Poopsie	R = Loopy
B = Lumpy	K = Flunky	S = Snotty
C = Buttercup	L = Booger	T = Falafel
D = Gidget	M = Pinky	U = Dorky
E = Crusty	N = Zippy	V = Squeezit
F = Greasy	O = Goober	W = Oprah
G = Fluffy	P = Doofus	X = Skipper
H = Cheeseball	Q = Slimy	Y = Dinky
I = Chim-Chim		Z = Zsa-Zsa

SECOND CHART: Use the first letter of your LAST NAME to determine the FIRST half of YOUR **NEW** Last Name.

A = Diaper	J = Monkey	R = Gizzard
B = Toilet	K = Potty	S = Pizza
C = Giggle	L = Liver	T = Gerbil
D = Bubble	M = Banana	U = Chicken
E = Girdle	N = Rhino	V = Pickle
F = Barf	O = Burger	W = Chuckle
G = Lizard	P = Hamster	X = Tofu
H = Waffle	Q = Toad	Y = Gorilla
I = Cootie		Z = Stinker

THIRD CHART: Use the LAST letter of your LAST NAME To determine the second half of your **NEW** Last Name.

A = Head	J = Honker	R = Buns
B = Mouth	K = Butt	S = Fanny
C = Face	L = Brain	T = Sniffer
D = Nose	M = Tushie	U = Sprinkles
E = Tush	N = Chunks	V = Kisser
F = Breath	O = Hiney	W = Squirt
G = Pants	P = Biscuits	X = Humperdinck
H = Shorts	Q = Toes	Y = Brains
I = Lips		Z = Juice

How to Set the Scene:

On sticker sheet #12, there are two poses of each hero.

A — Before contact.

B — CONTACT!

The Flip-O-Rama action pages are found behind sticker sheet #12. Decide who you want each hero to smack. Put the hero's A pose on page A, then the same hero's B pose on page B.

Add to the action with a few well-placed "pain stars" on page B, after the hero has made contact. And don't forget to add your own sound-effects!

ONCE YOU'VE SET THE SCENE,

HERE'S HOW iT WORKS

STEP 1

First, place your *left* hand inside the dotted lines marked "LEFT HAND HERE." Hold the book open *flat*.

STEP 2

Grasp the *right-hand* page with your right thumb and index finger (inside the dotted lines marked "RIGHT THUMB HERE").

STEP 3

Now *quickly* flip the right-hand page back and forth until the picture appears to be *animated*.

TRA·LA·LAAAA!

LEFT
HAND
HERE

RIGHT
INDEX
FINGER
HERE

CREDITS

CAPTAIN UNDERPANTS AND HIS WORLD CREATED BY DAV PILKEY

EDITORS: MICHAEL SHERMAN, CASSANDRA PELHAM, ANAMIKA BHATNAGAR

DESIGN: MICHAEL SHERMAN

GRAPHIC SUPPORT: QUILLON TSANG, DAN LETCHWORTH, JILL TURNEY, DAVID AVIDOR

BUYER/PLANNER: KELLY SHAFFER

PRODUCTION EDITOR: JEN MILLS